Stitched Paper Art

For Kids

22 *Cheeky Pickle* Sewing Projects

Ali Benyon

FunStitch
STUDIO
an imprint of C&T Publishing

Text copyright © 2014 by Ali Benyon

Photography and Artwork copyright © 2014 by C&T Publishing, Inc.

PUBLISHER: Amy Marson

CREATIVE DIRECTOR: Gailen Runge

ART DIRECTOR/COVER DESIGNER: Kristy Zacharias

EDITOR: S. Michele Fry

TECHNICAL EDITOR: Ann Haley

BOOK DESIGNER: April Mostek

PRODUCTION COORDINATORS: Zinnia Heinzmann and Freesia Pearson Blizard

PRODUCTION EDITOR: Katie Van Amburg

ILLUSTRATOR: Jessica Jenkins

PHOTO ASSISTANT: Mary Peyton Peppo

STYLED PHOTOS by Nissa Brehmer, unless otherwise noted;
INSTRUCTIONAL PHOTOS by Diane Pedersen, unless otherwise noted

Published by FunStitch Studio, an imprint of C&T Publishing, Inc., P.O. Box 1456, Lafayette, CA 94549

Library of Congress Cataloging-in-Publication Data

Benyon, Ali, 1973- author.
Stitched Paper Art for Kids : 22 cheeky pickle sewing projects / Ali Benyon.
    pages cm
Includes bibliographical references and index.
ISBN 978-1-60705-927-1 (soft cover : alk. paper)
1. Paper work. 2. Handicraft. 3. Stitches (Sewing) I. Title.

TT870.B465 2014
745.592--dc23

2014013068

Printed in China

10 9 8 7 6 5 4 3 2 1

Dedication

I'd like to dedicate this book to my gorgeous little family:
to my long-standing and loving husband, Dave,
and to my two beautiful girls, Madeleine and Greta.
What would I be without you all?

Acknowledgments

I'd like to thank all at C&T Publishing for asking me to write this book and for all their support along the way.

To my lovely circle of friends—you know who you all are—thanks for keeping me going through all my moaning and self-doubt. Massive thanks to my ever-supportive friend Elizabeth for giving me 1,001 ideas whenever I called and asked for help.

Finally, to Dave, Maddy, and Greta, who have put up with my being absent from them for far too many weekends, too many family day trips and family movie nights—apologies for my grumpiness over the last few months. I promise with all my heart to make it up to you all.

cheeky pickle
by ali benyon designs

Contents

Introduction

Why Do I Love Paper Stitch So Much?

Where do I start? OK, here goes! Stitching into paper is so much fun! It's a pretty easy, inexpensive, and quick way to create fabulous and one-of-a-kind projects. I'm so glad you have decided to join me in creating some gorgeous gifts and other goodies; we are going to have so much fun! So come on! What are we waiting for?

Think Unique, Not Perfect

I'm very enthusiastic about paper stitch—can you tell? Through this book, I hope to inspire you to be just as passionate as I am about paper and all the wonderful things you can create with it. Don't worry if you don't get it right the first time or you're thinking that yours doesn't look exactly like mine. That's totally fine! Remember, we learn through the mistakes we make, so make many—it's OK, honest! I've made loads of mistakes along the way; in fact, I still do—every day.

Just relax, experiment with different papers, and don't be scared to try out new techniques. Why not invite a friend along and get creative together? It's so much more fun when you can bounce your inventive and crazy ideas off each other.

What's in Store

First up, we'll talk about the basics you need to know: using a sewing machine, matching colors, choosing papers, tracing, and using patterns. Then I'll work closely with you and we'll take it nice and slowly, tiny step by tiny step, until you feel confident enough to go it alone. Trust me—it won't be long at all before you're whipping up your very own, totally awesome stitched-paper creations.

Come on, why are we hanging around here? Let's just go for it!

Just the Basics

Basic Sewing Terms

Craft supplies and techniques may have different names in different parts of the world. In this book, I've used the American terms. I am originally from England and now live in Australia. In this book, I added the terms I use in parentheses—let's hope you can understand me.

Appliqué: Merriam-Webster's dictionary says that *appliqué* is a *"cutout decoration fastened to a larger piece of material."* Appliqué is pretty much what you are doing when you stitch into paper. It doesn't matter that the material you're using is paper and not fabric. You are still appliquéing one material onto another, but you're using glue to stick it in place and a sewing machine to sew around it.

Backstitch: Most sewing machines have a button that will cause the machine to sew in reverse, creating this stitch. So find your machine's backstitch button.

Card stock: Card stock is smooth. It is thicker and heavier than construction paper, and the colors tend to be more vibrant and varied. You can substitute construction paper for some projects, but you will have a less smooth and less sturdy finished item.

Freezer paper (baking paper): This paper has a shiny side and a dull side. Place it on your table with the shiny side facing up. The patterned papers won't stick to it and you won't get glue on your nice table.

Pattern: A shape used when making something. For us, the patterns are what we will trace from the book.

Patterned: Something with a repeated artistic or decorative design. We will use patterned paper (paper with designs on it) for our projects.

Tracing paper: Thin, transparent paper that you put over a picture so that you can draw over its lines in order to make a copy of the picture.

Zigzag stitch: You know what a zigzag is. Well, most likely your machine will do this side-to-side stitch for you! Cool!

Threading a Machine

When you first have a go at threading your machine, you will probably find it a bit tricky. Don't worry! After you have done it a few times, you will manage to do it in seconds! Grab your instruction manual just in case. Most machines are threaded this way, so just carefully follow the arrows in the photo (at right) or the instructions in your machine's manual.

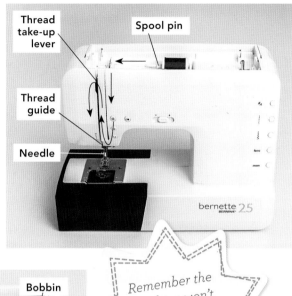

Thread take-up lever

Spool pin

Thread guide

Needle

bernette 25

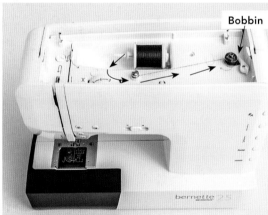

Bobbin

bernette 25

Remember the machine won't sew properly unless you thread it correctly and in this order.

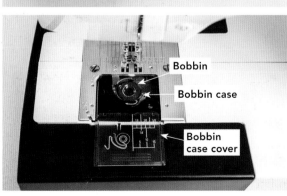

Bobbin

Bobbin case

Bobbin case cover

Also, don't forget that you will have to thread the bobbin, too. Wind the bobbin from the bobbin winder spindle. Then thread the bobbin into the bobbin case and insert it into the machine correctly. Double and triple check that you have done it properly before you start sewing. Good luck, guys!

Sewing on a Machine

Sewing on paper is much easier than sewing on fabric. In fact, it's a super-fun way for beginners to learn sewing machine basics. After just one project, I bet you'll be totally confident.

As you work your way through each project, I'll talk you through every step. Don't worry about a thing; we're in this together.

Things to Remember

1. Use a medium-sized needle.

2. Use a medium stitch length. (It's number 3 on my machine.) Stitches that are too short will rip the paper. Stitches that are too long will come loose.

Three stitch sizes. Use the middle one.

3. Use cotton rather than polyester thread. Make it bright! If you are using pink paper, use a green or blue cotton thread. It will stand out much better than a matching thread!

4. Use a medium-thick card stock. If the paper you use is too thin it will easily tear, too thick and you could break your needle! Experiment by buying a few pieces of paper that are of different thicknesses. You'll soon find out which ones work best for you.

Will My Needle Break?

People ask me all the time if I break needles a lot. In fact, nothing could be further from the truth: I have actually never broken a needle! However, paper will dull the needle quickly. Replace the sewing machine needle before sewing on fabric.

Securing Ends

Guess what—you don't always need to secure the ends of the thread, as you have to when sewing fabric. In fact, hardly ever! Just sew, cut the ends, and you're done. It couldn't be easier or quicker. However, once in a while I will tell you to backstitch something. That means it just needs that little extra stabilization.

Using Tracing Paper and Patterns

Using the patterns in this book is a really easy and simple way to create some cute designs for your projects. You can use these patterns for the project they are associated with or for other projects in the book. Mix it up!

Use your imagination and you will be amazed at all the different things you can make from just one pattern!

The first step of preparing to use a design will be tracing it from the book onto tracing paper.

Tracing Designs

1. -------------------------------
Place a sheet of tracing paper on top of the pattern you want to copy.

2. -------------------------------
Hold the tracing paper steady with your hand. Using a pencil, carefully trace on each line of the pattern.

3. -------------------------------
When you finish, turn the tracing paper over and place a piece of scrap paper under it so you don't get pencil marks on your table. Draw over the design again. Now the design is drawn on both sides of the tracing paper. The design you just drew is the mirror image of the original design. In this example, the branch is pointed in the opposite direction.

4. Trace the shapes you want to cut from each paper.

Now the shape is ready to cut out for your project. Easy!

Tip: If you don't have tracing paper at home, then try using freezer paper. It works very well. But, pssst—don't forget to ask permission to use it!

Storing Patterns

Keep your patterns safe by storing them all together in a special folder. Take your tracing papers with the designs on them and pop them into a folder or a binder with sleeve protectors. You could organize the binder into sections, such as love, animals, or flowers.

Creating Your Own Patterns

Once you get confident, build up a folder with your very own patterns. The choices are endless. What means something to you? What do you like? Find a picture of the shape or object you like and trace it. Or draw your design freehand like I did for the patterns in this book. Keep adding to your file every time an idea pops into your mind.

Color and Pattern

What I love most about stitching paper is the huge choice of patterned papers out there! Some of them are absolutely gorgeous. However, walking around a scrapbooking or paper shop for the first time might be a bit scary when you're faced with so much choice!

So I've come up with a few guidelines that will help you choose the right combination of papers. These tips will also keep you from spending too much money and make your projects look totally fantastic.

Color Tip: Don't worry too much. Most papers are available in sets, with all the hard work of color matching done for you! If in doubt, go and ask at your local scrapbooking or paper shop.

The Three-Color-and-Pattern Rule

When choosing papers, I always use the three-color-and-pattern rule. Try to stick to these simple instructions, and I promise you won't go far wrong. Let's get started.

1. Hunt down a totally amazing piece of patterned paper that you absolutely love and that hits you in the face when you see it. It has to have the "Wow!" factor, right?

2. Look closely at the paper and notice the 3 or 4 colors within the pattern that jump out at you. These are your accent colors.

The 3 colors that stand out with this paper are pink, brown, and turquoise.

3. Find some solid-color papers or some simple dotted or striped papers that match these accent colors. You should end up with 4 or 5 sheets of paper—a patterned sheet and 3 or 4 plainer pieces that look nice together. Use these papers in your project, and the finished result will look awesome. (Yes, if you end up with a patterned paper and only 2 plainer pieces, it will all still work out.)

These papers look cool together!

Supplies

What I love about all the projects in this book is that it's so easy to get started straight away. Other than the sewing machine, you won't need to spend lots of money on fancy, expensive materials, either. In fact, I bet you have most of them in your craft cupboard right now. So what are you waiting for? Go on; have a look, and let's get sewing. I know you're dying to.

Always Losing Your Craft Materials?

If you are, try storing them all together in a box (that you've made, of course), along with this book. Then everything you need is at hand. You'll be ready to start sewing and won't waste any time trying to find things.

Another handy organizer is a worker's toolbox. You can buy an inexpensive toolbox from a hardware store. It will have lots of compartments for storing all your materials. Bobbins, buttons, glue—there is a place for everything.

This is my toolbox. It's perfect for all your little **bits and bobs**. In England, that's what we call all your random little things, like buttons, thread, needles, and scissors.

Basic Supplies

You will need most of these things to make the projects.

Sewing machine

Sewing machine manual: Have a quick look through this. Familiarize yourself with the parts of the machine.

Colored threads and bobbins

Tracing paper

Patterned paper: This type of paper is often found in the scrapbook section of your craft store. It is usually heavier than ordinary paper. The really heavy paper is card stock. The instructions for each project will give you a suggested number of patterned papers to use. Most projects do not require heavyweight card stock, so look at the project supply list to see if you need it.

Glue stick

White craft glue (PVA glue)

Pencil

Scissors: small scissors for cutting thread and large scissors for cutting paper

Tracing paper or freezer paper

Supplies That Come in Handy for Some Projects

See the supply list for each project.

Pinking shears: for cutting paper with lovely patterned edges

Ruler

Buttons

Clear plastic or vinyl

Ribbon or twine

Beads

Freezer paper (baking paper)

Paintbrush

Small hole punch

Shaped paper punch: for instance, hearts or flowers, at least 1½˝ in width

Sequins

Stick-on jewels (diamantés)

Fabric scraps

Clear adhesive tape (Sellotape)

Hook-and-loop tape

Washi tape

Notes

The instructions for each project will tell you whether you should use a glue stick or white glue.

Some projects work better with heavier card stock. I will let you know if you need it.

The Perfect Gift

Bookmark

Who doesn't love a surprise? If you're buying a book for someone special, why not pop one of these lovely handmade bookmarks inside as an extra surprise gift? You can also use other patterns in this book to make ones to suit all your friends and family. What about a flower bookmark for Mum, a butterfly for Auntie, or a heart one for Dad to show how much you care? Now that would be awesome!

Project Supply List

For a list of general sewing supplies, see Basic Supplies (page 14).

❋ **For the birdhouse front, roof, and flower:** 4 patterned papers

❋ **For front of bookmark rectangle A:** 1 patterned paper

❋ **For back of birdhouse and rectangle B:** 1 solid-color heavy card stock

❋ **Narrow ribbon:** 4 pieces, each 12″ long

❋ **1 button**

Let's Get Making!

1. Trace the bookmark patterns (page 19) onto various patterned papers. Cut the shapes out. Trace and cut another birdhouse shape from heavy plain card stock. Cut a 2½″ × 9″ rectangle A from the patterned paper. Cut another 2½″ × 9″ piece from the heavy plain card stock for rectangle B.

2. Stick all the paper birdhouse pieces onto the solid-colored heavy card stock birdhouse, using a glue stick.

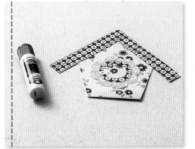

3. Before the glue dries, lift the lower edge of the flower in the center and slip the ends of the 4 ribbons under the edge.

4. Use the glue stick to stick rectangle A on top of rectangle B.

5. Sew A and B together around the outside edges.

Tip: I like to sew wavy lines to add extra pattern and texture.

6.

Sew around the edge of the birdhouse. Use a zigzag stitch along the roof to add a little effect. Don't forget to sew a few times around the flower to hold that pretty ribbon in place.

You're almost there.

7. Slide the end of the bookmark rectangle under the birdhouse so the 2 pieces overlap by about 1″. Push the ribbons aside, then sew across the bottom edge of the birdhouse. Finish off with a zigzag stitch just above the straight stitches.

8. Add a big, bright button to the center of the flower with a little white glue.

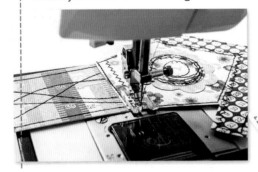

All finished! Give with love!

Stitched Paper Art for Kids

Refer to *Using Tracing Paper and Patterns* (page 10) for help with tracing and cutting pattern shapes.

1. Cut 1 birdhouse (bold lines), 1 roof, 1 flower, 1 small circle, and 1 large circle from various patterned papers.

2. Cut 1 birdhouse (bold lines) from heavy plain card stock.

Roof

Flower

Large circle

Small circle

Bunting Necklace

These bunting necklaces are quick and easy to make. They are perfect for brightening up a new dress or as a great last-minute gift. This project can seem a little tricky at first, so have a practice on some scrap bunting shapes first.

Project Supply List

For a list of general sewing supplies, see Basic Supplies (page 14).

❋ **For bunting shapes:** 2 patterned papers

❋ **Colored twine:** 30″ piece

❋ **4 buttons**

❋ **Freezer paper** (baking paper)

❋ **Paintbrush**

Let's Get Making!

1. Trace the bunting pattern (page 23) and cut out the shapes from various patterned papers. Cut 5 pieces total.

2. Measure 11″ from 1 end of the twine. This is where the first bunting shape will go.

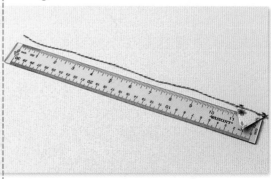

3.

Place the twine on top of the bunting, and sew slowly over the twine, using a zigzag stitch. Make sure the twine is in the center of the stitch. Sew halfway across the first bunting piece, and then back-stitch to keep it in place.

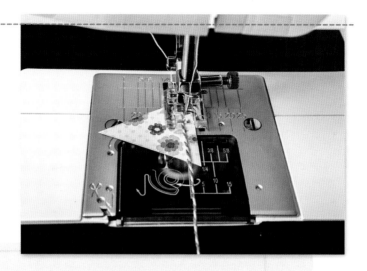

Tip: For this project, it's best if you use a thread that matches the color of your paper bunting. That way if you make any mistakes, no one will notice.

4.

Take your next section of bunting and place it under the twine, next to the first bunting section. Continue to stitch until all 5 bunting pieces are in place. When you get to the last bunting, backstitch to make it extra secure. Trim any stray threads.

5.

Thread 2 buttons on each end of the twine. Slide the buttons so they are near the bunting pieces.

6.

Place the necklace on the shiny side of the freezer paper. Using a small paintbrush from your toolbox, paste a thin layer of white glue all over the paper bunting. Once dry, turn over and paste the other side.

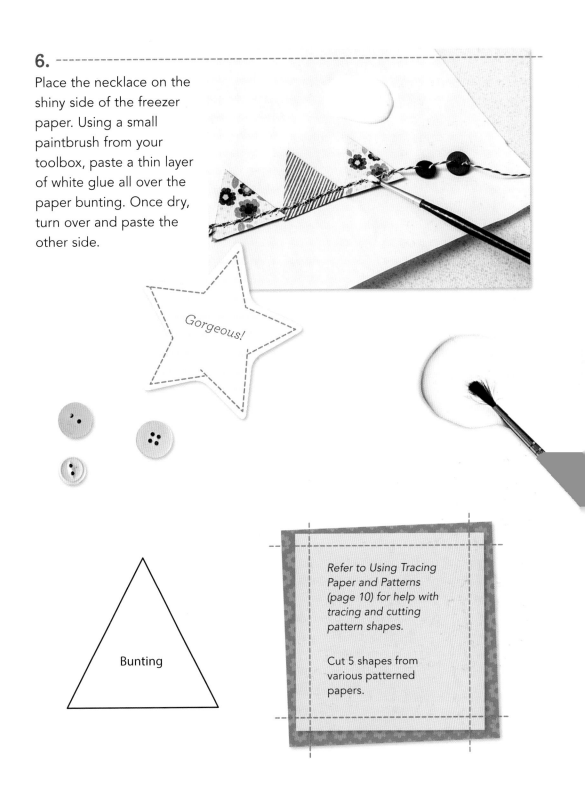

Gorgeous!

Bunting

Refer to Using Tracing Paper and Patterns (page 10) for help with tracing and cutting pattern shapes.

Cut 5 shapes from various patterned papers.

Flower Necklace

These dainty little flower necklaces remind me of warm summer evenings and make me feel so happy! Make one for someone special using all her favorite colors, and I promise she will love you forever. I've used wooden beads for mine, but there are so many kinds of beads to choose from—glass, plastic, shiny, tiny, or huge ones. It's your project, so you choose!

Project Supply List

For a list of general sewing supplies, see Basic Supplies (page 14).

- ❄ **For flowers:** 3 patterned papers

- ❄ **Colored ribbon:** 30″ piece

- ❄ **10–12 small beads**

- ❄ **Button**

- ❄ **Hole punch**

- ❄ **Clear adhesive tape** (Sellotape)

Let's Get Making!

1. Trace and cut out 1 flower, 1 small circle, and 1 large circle using the flower pattern (page 27).

2. ----------------------------
Using a glue stick, glue the large circle shape onto the flower. Glue the small circle to the center of the large circle.

3.

With a bold, contrasting thread, sew around the circles 3 or 4 times.

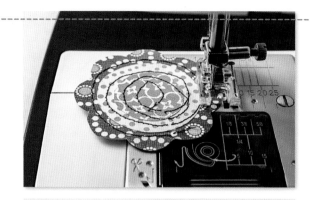

4.

Cut a 1″ straight line from the outer edge to the center of the flower.

5.

Overlap the cut edges and tape them securely together on the outside. Just use a little bit of tape. You don't want it to show on the front.

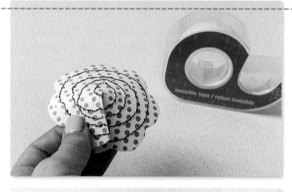

6.

Punch 2 small holes about ¼″ apart near the center of the flower.

7. Thread the ribbon through the 2 holes. Slide the flower to the center of the ribbon.

8. Tie a knot in the ribbon on either side of the flower, near the holes.

Tie knots to secure the ribbon.

9.

Add beads to each end of the ribbon. Put 5 or 6 beads on either side of the flower. Tie a knot 1˝ from the last bead on each side to stop the beads from coming off the end.

You're all finished. Well done, you! Your mum or bestie will just love it!

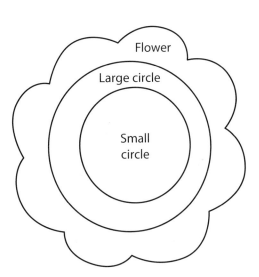

Flower

Large circle

Small circle

Refer to Using Tracing Paper and Patterns (page 10) for help with tracing and cutting pattern shapes.

Cut 1 flower, 1 large circle, and 1 small circle from patterned papers.

Butterfly Brooch

I personally think you can never have enough jewelry! And I bet all your friends will be totally amazed when you give them one of these gorgeous butterfly brooches. Make them nice and bright so that your friends really stand out from the crowd, and then be proud when you tell everyone that you made it! You can try making a brooch with the other patterns as well—the flower, maybe, or even a cute little house brooch!

Project Supply List

For a list of general sewing supplies, see Basic Supplies (page 14).

* **For butterfly:**
  2 patterned papers

* **kraft•tex***

* **1 safety pin:** about 1½″ long

* **Twill tape or heavy fabric:**
  2 pieces 1″ × ½″ each

* **Small stick-on jewels (diamantés) or sequins**

* **Paintbrush**

*What is kraft•tex?

kraft•tex is a fabulous and really handy product to have in your craft cupboard. I love using it! It's a rugged paper that looks and feels like leather. However, it's strong and washable like fabric! You can do all kinds of projects with it, and it works perfectly with paper. However, if you use it with other papers, don't wash it! It's a C&T Publishing product. Check your local craft stores or go online at ctpub.com. (Don't order anything without getting adult permission!)

Let's Get Making!

Go on—grab some really bright and funky papers for this project!

1.

Trace and cut out 1 small and 1 large butterfly from the patterned papers, using the pattern (page 31).

2.

Stick the small butterfly onto the center of the large butterfly, using a glue stick.

3.

Using the large butterfly pattern, cut out another butterfly from the kraft•tex.

4.

Glue the kraft•tex butterfly to the back of the paper butterfly.

5.

Sew around each of the butterflies 3 times to make a pretty pattern. Trim off any stray threads.

6. --

Using white glue and a paintbrush, adhere 1 piece of twill tape to the back of the butterfly. Place the open safety pin on top (make sure the sharp pin point is sticking up).

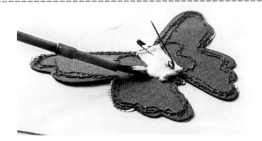

7. --

Glue the other piece of fabric across the pin, as shown. Spread the glue over the top of the fabric and leave it to dry completely.

8. --

Finish off your brooch with style by adding some shimmer and shine. Add a few jewels with a dab of white glue.

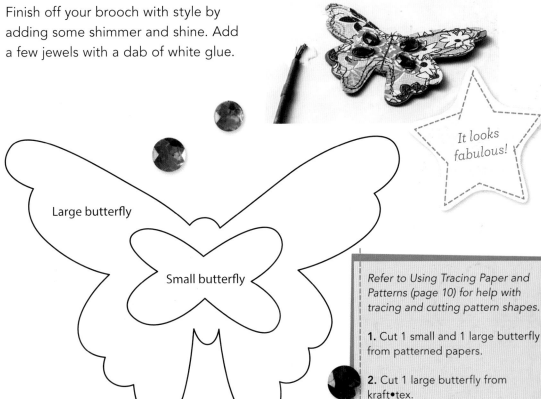

Large butterfly

Small butterfly

It looks fabulous!

Refer to *Using Tracing Paper and Patterns* (page 10) for help with tracing and cutting pattern shapes.

1. Cut 1 small and 1 large butterfly from patterned papers.

2. Cut 1 large butterfly from kraft•tex.

Flower Headband

Before you start on these funky headbands, you might want to secretly find out what your friend's favorite outfit is. Then you can search for some gorgeous papers that will match it. She will absolutely love you for it! We are using hook-and-loop tape for this project. You can find it easily at your local craft store, and it's really useful to have in your toolbox!

Project Supply List

For a list of general sewing supplies, see Basic Supplies (page 14).

✾ **2–4 patterned papers** (You will only need 2 papers if your paper has a design on the back as well as the front.)

✾ **Headband**

✾ **Self-adhesive hook-and-loop tape:** 1˝ piece

✾ **Twine or narrow ribbon:** 8˝ piece

✾ **1 button**

✾ **Clear adhesive tape** (Sellotape)

✾ **Hole punch:** to make ⅛˝-wide holes (*optional*)

Let's Get Making!

1. Trace and cut 1 large flower, 1 small flower, 1 large circle, and 1 small circle using the patterns (page 36).

2. Using a glue stick, glue the circle shapes onto the smaller flower.

3. With a bright, contrasting thread, sew around the flower 3 or 4 times.

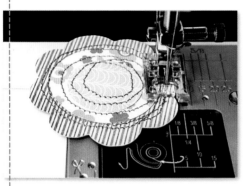

4. Stitch around the larger flower.

5. Cut a straight line about 1″ toward the center of the small flower. Fold the cut edges toward each other so they overlap a little bit. Tape the edges together securely on the outside of the flower.

Cut.

Fold.

Tape.

6. Punch a small hole in the center of the small flower. You could use a pencil if you don't have a hole punch. Make a small hole in the center of the large flower, too.

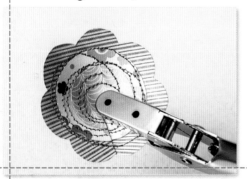

7.

Thread the twine through the hole in the small flower from the back to the front. Thread it through 1 buttonhole from back to front also. Now reverse the process: Push the twine through the other buttonhole from front to back. Go back through the hole in the small flower.

8.

Thread both tails through the hole in the large flower. Tug gently on the thread so the button sits snugly in the middle of the small flower. Tie a knot at the back of the large flower—not too tight or the paper will rip! Using white glue, stick the small flower to the large flower. Let dry. Remember, it won't stick flat. The glue is just to hold it in place.

9. When the glue is completely dry, trim the twine tails. Stick a side of a piece of hook-and-loop tape onto the back of the flower. Wrap the other side around the headband, where you want the flower to go.

10.

Attach the flower to your headband.

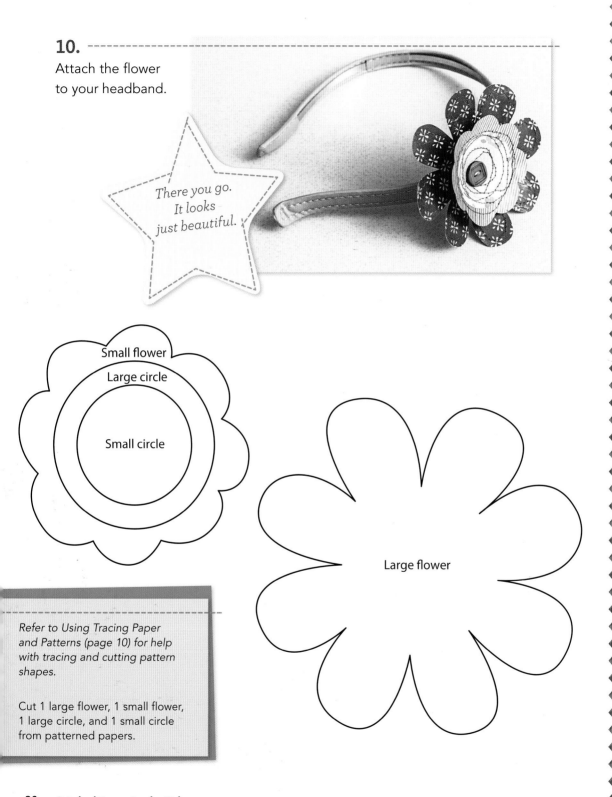

There you go. It looks just beautiful.

Small flower

Large circle

Small circle

Large flower

Refer to Using Tracing Paper and Patterns (page 10) for help with tracing and cutting pattern shapes.

Cut 1 large flower, 1 small flower, 1 large circle, and 1 small circle from patterned papers.

Get Organized!

Bag Tag

Project Supply List

For a list of general sewing supplies, see Basic Supplies (page 14).

- ❊ 2 or 3 patterned papers
- ❊ kraft•tex
- ❊ 2 pieces of clear vinyl: 6″ × 6″ each
- ❊ 1 hinged metal ring

These bag tags are a great way to dress up a boring old school bag. Add your name and address details, too, to keep it safe. You can encase almost anything in there; why not try a dried flower, a leaf, or a photo of you and your best friend!

Let's Get Making!

1.

Trace and cut out 1 small flower, 1 large flower, 2 large circles, and 1 small circle from the papers, using the patterns (page 43). Then cut 1 large circle from the kraft•tex. Also, cut a strip of kraft•tex ½″ × 3″.

Daisy
Jones
Class 3B

2.

Use a glue stick to glue the small circle to the center of the large flower. Then glue the large flower to a large circle.

3.

Glue the small flower to the other large circle. Write your name and address in the center of this flower.

4.

Stitch around the large and small flowers. Make a nice design around your name if you like!

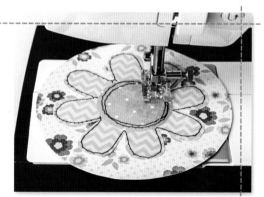

5. Glue the circles together with the kraft•tex circle between them. Stick the top flower onto the kraft•tex using a glue stick. Turn it over, and then stick the other flower onto it.

6.

Take the 1½˝ × 3˝ strip of kraft•tex and fold it in half. Then pop it between the flowers, so the folded end sticks out about 1˝.

7.

Place a piece of the vinyl on each side, over the large and small flowers.

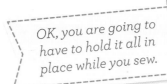

OK, you are going to have to hold it all in place while you sew.

8.

Sew around the flower.
Make sure the folded strip
of kraft•tex is secure, and
stitch it in place as well.

9.

Cut off the excess vinyl
around the circle, leaving
an edge of about ¼˝ around
the outside of it. Attach the
metal ring to the folded
kraft•tex, and you're
finished! Hooray!

Large circle

Small flower

Large flower

Small circle

Refer to Using Tracing Paper and Patterns (page 10) for help with tracing and cutting pattern shapes.

Cut 1 large flower, 1 small flower, 1 small circle, and 2 large circles from patterned papers.

Cut 1 large circle from kraft•tex.

Covered Notebook

Your gorgeous, paper-covered notebooks will bring oohs and aahs! This project can be a little bit tricky, but you'll be proud of it when you're done. Go ahead and get a friend on board to help!

Let's Get Making!

1. On the wrong side (the side you want on the inside of the notebook cover) of the back paper, measure 3″ in from the left 10¼″ edge. Mark it with a pencil.

Project Supply List

For a list of general sewing supplies, see Basic Supplies (page 14).

- ❋ **2–4 medium- or heavy-weight patterned papers cut to the following sizes*:**

  9¾″ × 10¼″ for front

  12½″ × 10¼″ for back

  2 strips, ½″ × 10¼″ each, for stripes

  4 hearts (See pattern, page 47.)

- ❋ **4 buttons**

- ❋ **Composition notebook:** 7½″ × 9¾″ (or A5 notebook*)

* For an A5 notebook (approximately 14.8cm × 21cm), cut cards to the following dimensions: 21cm × 23cm for front, 27cm × 23cm for back, and 2 strips 1.4cm × 23cm for stripes.

2.

Mark the wrong side of the front paper, but this time measure 3˝ in from the *right* 10¼˝ edge. Draw a line with a pencil.

3. With a ruler, fold the back piece in at the mark to make a flap. Do the same with the front piece. Turn both pieces over.

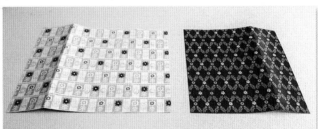

4.

Glue the ½˝ × 10¼˝ stripes to the front card, just left of the crease. Glue the hearts on top of the stripes. Sew along the stripes using a zigzag stitch.

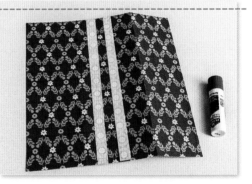

5.

Glue the front and the back together, overlapping by ¼″. Sew a straight line all the way down along the overlapped edges.

6.

Turn the cover over and stitch along the top and bottom edges. Sew near the edges, making sure the folded flaps are sewn down.

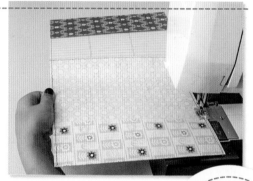

7. Glue the buttons to the hearts, using white glue. Leave to dry.

Phew! Now doesn't that look fantastic?

8. Slide a composition notebook into the cover.

Heart

Refer to Using Tracing Paper and Patterns (page 10) for help with tracing and cutting pattern shapes.

Cut 4 hearts from patterned paper.

Difficulty level: 🔘

Storage Box

These storage boxes are a great way to keep all your bits and bobs neat and tidy. You could also take the same idea and decorate a mirror, a clock, or a jewelry box!

Project Supply List

For a list of general sewing supplies, see Basic Supplies (page 14).

❋ **4 (or more) patterned papers** (See Tip, below.)

❋ **kraft•tex:** about 14″ × 16″

❋ **8 small buttons**

❋ **Small box with a lid** (The one I used is 6″ × 6″ × 3¼″.)

❋ **Paintbrush**

Tip: Don't forget you can use my guide in Color and Pattern (page 12) to help you choose some awesome combinations!

Let's Get Making!

1.

Using the patterns (page 53), trace and cut out 8 roofs, 8 house shapes, 8 windows, and 8 doors. Glue a window and a door to each of the houses, using a glue stick.

2.

Cut out 8 roof and 8 house shapes from the kraft•tex. If you don't have kraft•tex, use heavy card stock.

3.

Sew around the windows and doors of each house.

4.

Glue the paper roofs to the kraft•tex roofs, using a glue stick. Sew around the edge of each roof.

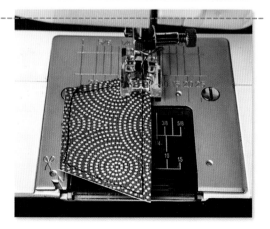

5. Glue the back of each patterned paper house to a kraft•tex house. Sew around the edge of each house.

6.

Use a paintbrush to spread white glue on the back of a house and place it on the outside of your box. Glue 2 houses on each side of the box.

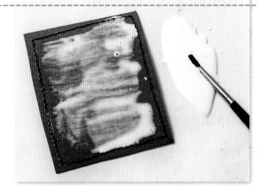

7.

Repeat Step 6 with the roofs, but glue them around the *lid* of the box.

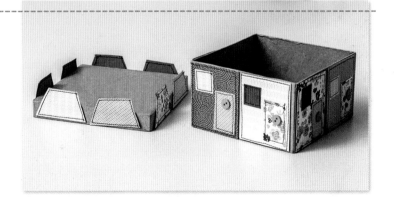

8. Leave the box and lid apart until dry.

9.

Finish the houses by using white glue to attach the buttons for door handles.

10. Trace and cut out 4 flower shapes, 4 large circles, and 4 small circles, using the flower pattern (page 36). Glue 1 flower, 1 large circle, and 1 small circle together, using a glue stick. Repeat to make 4 flowers. Sew around each flower.

11.

Use white glue to attach each flower to the lid. Add some buttons to make a pretty design.

Now you've got a super place to hide all your secret things!

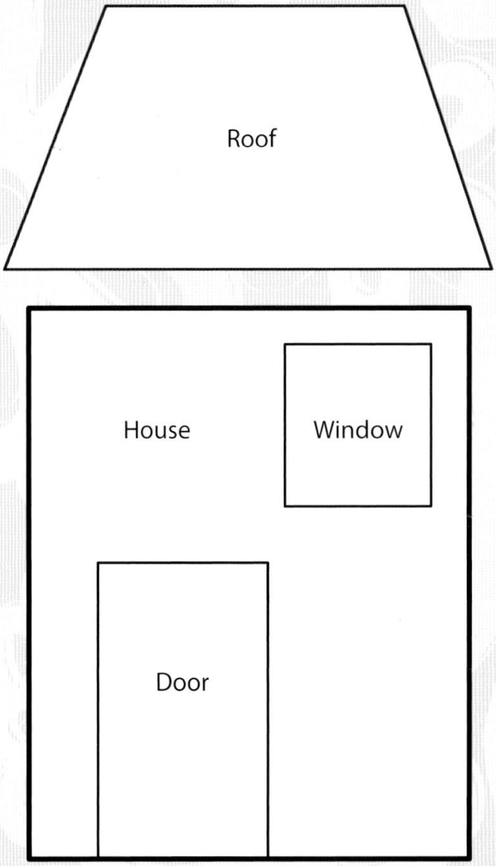

Roof

House

Window

Door

Refer to Using Tracing Paper and Patterns (page 10) for help with tracing and cutting pattern shapes.

Cut 8 roofs, 8 doors, 8 windows, and 8 house rectangles (using the bold lines) from patterned papers.

Cut 8 roofs and 8 house rectangles (using the bold lines) from kraft•tex.

For decorative flowers, see the flower pattern (page 36). Cut 4 flowers, 4 large circles, and 4 small circles from patterned papers.

Storage Hanger

We are going to use pieces of vinyl for this fantastic storage project. Hold on tight for some creative and super-fun sewing!

Let's Get Making!

1. Glue the 3 long strips of patterned paper (pieces B) on top of the long strip of kraft•tex (piece A) using a glue stick. Sew all the way around the outside of the long strip, about ¼″ in from the edge. Add a few extra stitched lines down the center.

Project Supply List

For a list of general sewing supplies, see Basic Supplies (page 14).

❊ **5 patterned papers**

Cut 3 strips of patterned paper 2″ × 12″ (piece B).

Cut 5 squares of patterned paper 5″ × 5″ (piece D).

Cut 5 hearts from patterned papers (see heart pattern, page 59).

❊ **8″ × 36″ piece of kraft•tex**

Cut 1 strip of kraft•tex 2″ × 36″ (piece A).

Cut 5 squares of kraft•tex 5″ × 5″ (piece C).

❊ **5 pieces of vinyl*:** *6″ × 6″ each*

❊ **Hole punch**

❊ **Ribbon:** *12″ piece*

** You can usually find vinyl or plastic at the craft store. I get mine from my local **haberdashery store**. (In Australia, this is a shop that sells thread, fabric, and other sewing supplies.)*

C&T Publishing (ctpub.com) makes Quilter's Vinyl, which works well for this project. In a pinch, you could use a plastic sheet protector, though it may not be quite as sturdy as vinyl.

2.

Using a glue stick, attach a paper square D to each kraft•tex square C. Space these squares evenly on the long strip, starting about 2″ from the top. Glue the squares in place with the glue stick.

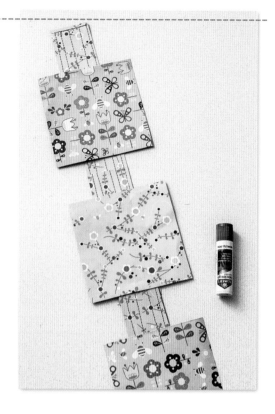

3. Sew across the top and bottom of each square. Sew only the part that is glued to the long strip. When you get to the edge, go back over the stitching again.

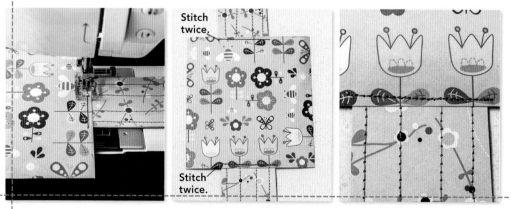

Stitch twice.

Stitch twice.

4. Center 1 of the hearts behind a piece of vinyl. Sew around the heart.

 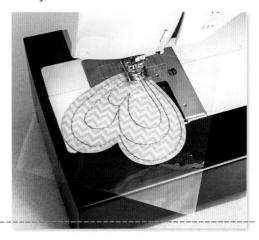

5. Repeat Step 4 for the rest of the hearts.

Have fun! Stitch a pretty design if you want and try to make each heart a little bit different.

6.

Place a vinyl heart piece on each of the paper squares. The vinyl is bigger than the paper square, so it will stick out a little bit on each side. Carefully sew along the side and bottom edges of each paper square. Stitching only 3 sides of each square will create pockets, so don't forget to leave the top part open!

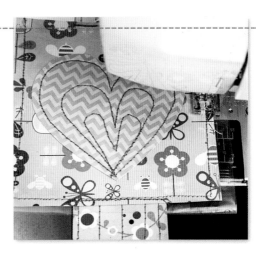

7.

Carefully trim the extra vinyl on the outer edges of each square.

Ta-da! Five pockets for bits and bobs.

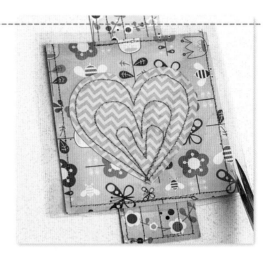

8. Punch a hole in the top of the storage hanger. Thread the ribbon through the hole to finish.

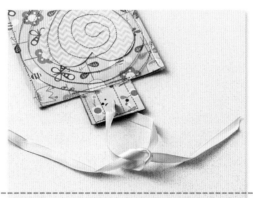

Heart

Refer to Using Tracing
Paper and Patterns
(page 10) for help with
tracing and cutting
pattern shapes.

Cut 5 hearts from various
patterned papers.

Difficulty level: 🔘 🔘

Tote Bag

This tote bag is super-cute and so handy for carrying all your bits and bobs.

Project Supply List

For a list of general sewing supplies, see Basic Supplies (page 14).

❀ **3 patterned papers**

❀ **kraft•tex: 14″ × 24″**

kraft•tex

This is a perfect project for kraft•tex (like the Hexagon Purse, page 64) because kraft•tex is strong like fabric and can stand up to lots of use. Bags and totes get plenty of hands-on use!

Let's Get Making!

1. Cut out 2 rectangles from kraft•tex, each 10″ × 11½″. These pieces will be the front and back of the tote bag.

2. Cut 12″-long wavy strips from the patterned papers. Cut 5 strips from each of your papers. You should have 15 strips total.

3. Glue the wavy paper strips to a rectangle of kraft•tex, using a glue stick. Don't worry if they overlap. That makes your design more interesting.

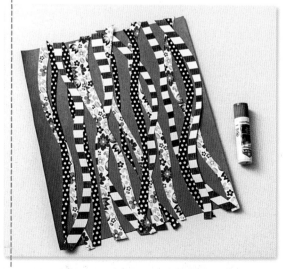

4.

Sew up and down the wavy lines. If you sew off the paper, that's fine. The more lines the better! Trim the ends of the paper strips if needed, and trim any stray threads. If you want to, you can also decorate the back of the bag with strips or stitching.

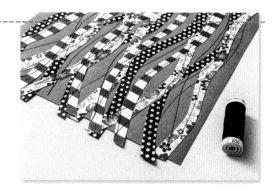

5.

Cut 2 strips of kraft•tex and 2 strips of patterned paper, each 1¼″ × 12″. These will be the handles. Glue a paper strip to each kraft•tex strip.

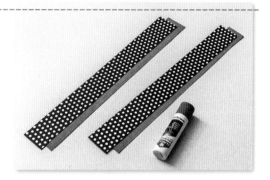

6.

Sew around the edges of the strips. Add a zigzag stitch down the center of each strip.

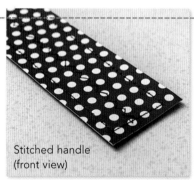

Stitched handle
(front view)

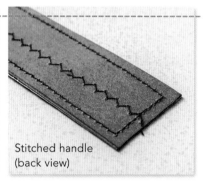

Stitched handle
(back view)

7.

Place 1 end of a handle strip under the top edge of the bag front (the kraft•tex piece with the wavy papers). The strip should be about 2½″ in from the top left corner of the bag front. Sew a rectangle shape where the bag overlaps the end of the handle. Stitch around the rectangle twice to make it secure.

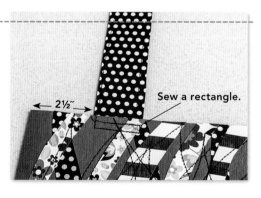

← 2½″ →

Sew a rectangle.

8.

Bend the strip into a U shape to make the handle, and sew the other end as you did in Step 7.

9.

Repeat Steps 7 and 8 to add the other handle to the other kraft•tex rectangle from Step 1. This will be the back of the tote bag.

10.

Place the front and back of the bag together. The ends of each handle should be on the inside. Sew ¼″ from the side and bottom edges of the bag. Don't forget to leave an opening at the top, though! Cut a small curve for each of the bottom corners. Be careful so you don't cut the stitches.

Hexagon Purse

Project Supply List

For a list of general sewing supplies, see Basic Supplies (page 14).

❋ 2 patterned papers

❋ kraft•tex

❋ Self-adhesive hook-and-loop tape: ½″ piece

❋ 1 button: about ½″ wide

These little purses are a fab idea for storing all sorts of things: money, hair clips, lip gloss. You name it, you can store it! In addition, with all the amazing choices of papers out there, you could have a different one for every day of the week!

Let's Get Making!

1.

Trace and cut out the pieces using the Hexagon Purse pattern (page 68) as follows:

- 1 full hexagon from the patterned paper
- 1 full hexagon from the kraft•tex
- 1 half-hexagon from the patterned paper
- 1 half-hexagon shape from the kraft•tex

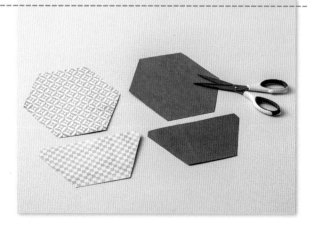

2. --

Glue the kraft•tex pieces to the backs of the similar paper pieces.

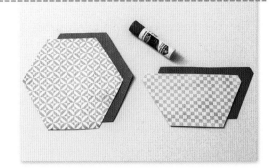

3. --

Fold the full hexagon shape over and make a crease. Use the top edge of the half-hexagon pattern (page 68) to show you where to fold. The smaller part of the folded hexagon will be the purse flap. After you make the crease, unfold the hexagon for now.

4. --

Sew along the long edge of the half-hexagon.

Sew along the top of the smaller shape.

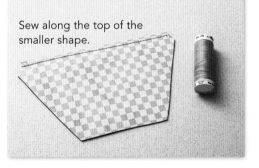

5. --

Place the half-hexagon on top of the full hexagon, so the kraft•tex pieces are on the inside, as shown. Sew all around the edge of the full hexagon.

Stitch.

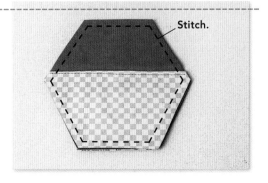

6.

Turn the purse over and sew zigzag stitches across the flap, if you like.

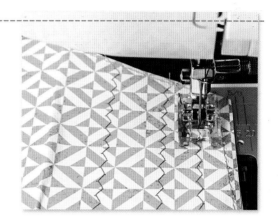

7.

Stick a side of the hook-and-loop tape to each part of the purse. Make sure that they will meet when the flap is folded!

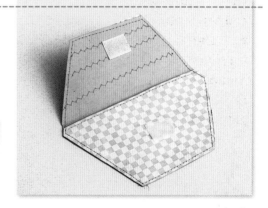

 Note

Hook-and-loop tape has 2 parts. One side has little tiny hooks all over it and the other side has little loops. Keep the parts together until you are ready to use them.

8.

Add a button to the front of the flap with a little bit of white glue, and you're finished.

Store all your personal little things in there!

Full hexagon
(bold outer lines)

Half-hexagon

*Refer to Using Tracing Paper and Patterns (page 10)
for help with tracing and cutting pattern shapes.*

Cut 1 full hexagon (bold outer lines) and
1 half-hexagon from patterned papers.

Cut 1 full hexagon (bold outer lines) and
1 half-hexagon from kraft•tex.

Let's Celebrate!

Greeting Card

Project Supply List

For a list of general sewing supplies, see Basic Supplies (page 14).

❋ **3 patterned papers**

❋ **White card stock:** Cut a 5½″ × 11″ rectangle and a 5½″ × 5½″ square.

Nothing could be nicer than a handmade, stitched card. So simple but effective! Just imagine the huge smile when the person opens this beautiful apple card that you've lovingly made just for them! My apple pattern is just an example of what you can do. What about hearts for Valentine's Day, an owl for a clever friend's birthday, or a stocking for Christmas?

Tip: When you are designing your cards, go for a simple shape. You don't have much room to work with, and a small but bold image will stand out strikingly!

Let's Get Making!

1.

Trace and cut out the apple pieces from 3 different patterned papers, using the apple pattern (page 73). Stick the apple shapes to the 5½″ × 5½″ card stock piece, using a glue stick.

2. With a dark brown thread, slowly sew around each part of the apple. Turn the stitched apple over and trim off the loose threads.

Tip: Use a bold-colored thread. The stitch will stand out beautifully and really show off your design!

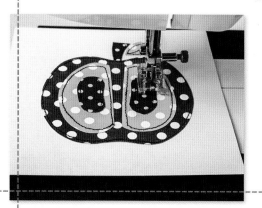

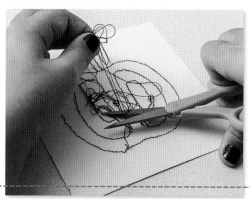

3.

Fold the 5½″ × 11″ card stock piece in half. Dab some glue on the back of the square card stock piece (with the apple on it), and stick it to the front of the folded card stock piece.

4.

Rethread the machine with white thread. The bobbin needs changing, too! Now carefully sew in a straight line all the way around the 5½″ × 5½″ card. Then trim off any loose threads.

It's finished. Send it with love!

Apple

Refer to Using Tracing Paper and Patterns (page 10) for help with tracing and cutting pattern shapes.

Cut 1 of each shape in the apple from your patterned papers.

Christmas Decorations

These little Christmas decorations are so cute! They can be a little bit tricky to make, so you might need an extra pair of hands to help!

Project Supply List

For a list of general sewing supplies, see Basic Supplies (page 14).

❋ Lightweight solid-color paper: 2 pieces 1½″ × 12″ each (piece A)

❋ Patterned paper: 2 pieces 1″ × 12″ each (piece B)

❋ Patterned paper: 2 pieces ¾″ × 8″ each (piece C)

❋ Patterned paper: 1 piece ½″ × 6½″ (piece D)

❋ Twine: 12″ piece

❋ Hole punch

Let's Get Making!

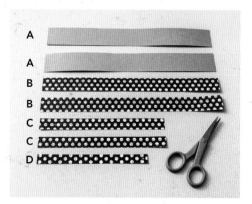

1. Glue a B piece to each A piece, as shown.

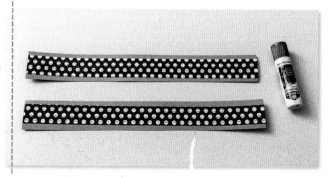

2.

Stitch around the edge of each piece from Step 1. Add a zigzag stitch down the center of each strip.

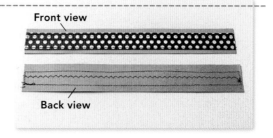

Front view

Back view

3.

Hold a C piece on top of a stitched piece from Step 2, as shown. The stitched piece should be face down, and the C piece should be face up (so you can see the paper's pattern). Make sure the ends meet at the bottom.

4. Gently fold the short strip of paper (C) toward you so that a small teardrop shape is formed. Then fold the long strip toward you to form a larger teardrop shape. Keep a tight hold on the ends!

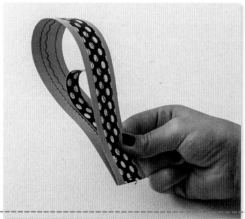

5.

Sew across the ends in a straight line. Backstitch to make sure they stay together.

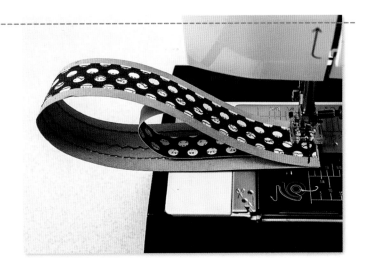

6.

Repeat Steps 3–5 with the other stitched piece and C piece. Trim off any loose threads.

7.

Place the D piece on top of 1 of the teardrop shapes.

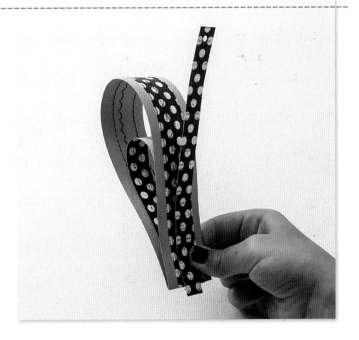

8.

Place the other teardrop shape on top so the D piece is between the teardrop shapes. The D piece should stick out just a little at the bottom.

9.

Sew across the bottom through all the layers, and backstitch to secure. Make sure all the layers are held together with the stitches. Trim the D piece at the bottom so all the edges are even.

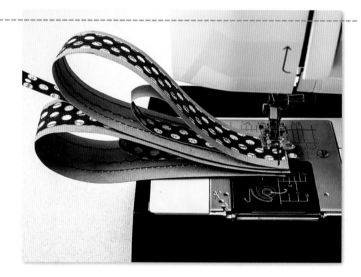

10.

Use a hole punch to make a small hole at the top of the D piece.

11.

Thread the twine through the hole and tie a small knot.

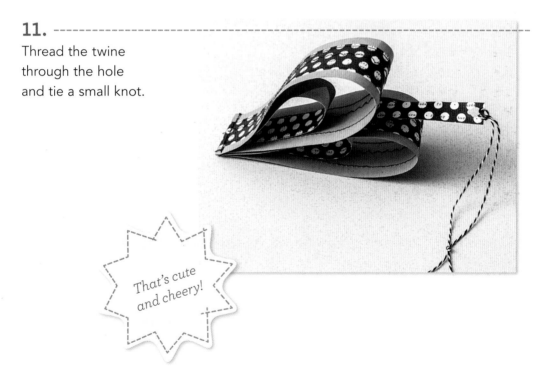

That's cute and cheery!

Difficulty level:

Gift Tag

Project Supply List

For a list of general sewing supplies, see Basic Supplies (page 14).

* ❋ 3 patterned papers

* ❋ **Heavyweight, solid-color card stock:** 2 pieces 3½˝ × 4˝ each

* ❋ **Narrow ribbon or twine:** 8˝ piece

* ❋ 3 sequins

* ❋ **Hole punch**

How cute is this gorgeous little gift tag? It simply shouts out that you really do care for the person you are giving it to. Nothing could be more thoughtful than a little bit of handmade!

It doesn't have to be a cupcake like I've done! Maybe you would like to try a candle for a Hanukkah present or a little bunny rabbit for your favorite niece or nephew at Easter time. Instead of using twine, you could use some gorgeous, shiny ribbon, too.

Let's Get Making!

1.

Trace and cut out the cupcake pieces, using the pattern (page 83). Glue the pieces to the center of a piece of card stock, using a glue stick.

2.

Slowly sew around the cupcake. Use a zigzag stitch along the top of the cupcake base. Turn the card over, and trim off any loose threads.

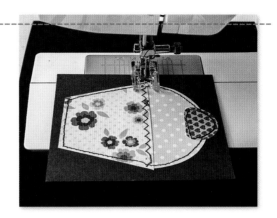

3.

Glue the back of the card stock from Step 2 to the other piece of colored card stock, using a glue stick. Make sure all the edges line up!

4.

Sew around the edges of the card stock. Use a matching thread for this part. Trim any loose threads.

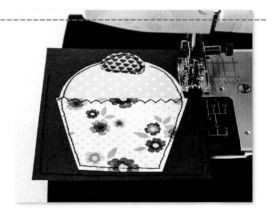

5.

Using a hole punch, punch a hole about ½″ from the top corner of the card stock.

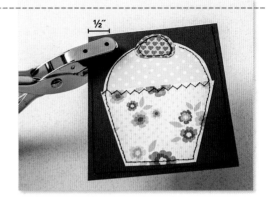

6.

Add a few sequins with a dab of white glue. Sequins will make the tag shimmer and shine. Now you're ready to add the ribbon and put it on your gift!

Wow, now doesn't that look just lovely?

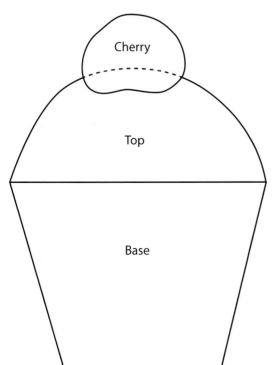

Cherry

Top

Base

Refer to Using Tracing Paper and Patterns (page 10) for help with tracing and cutting pattern shapes.

Cut 1 cupcake base, 1 cupcake top, and 1 cherry shape from various patterned papers.

Wrapping Paper

This gorgeous, handmade wrapping paper is just so pretty that your friends won't ever want to throw it away! There are so many different designs and patterns you could try, too. What about hearts and buttons, shiny metallic thread, or even strips of satin ribbon? I'm too excited! Come on, let's get started!

Project Supply List

For a list of general sewing supplies, see Basic Supplies (page 14).

❋ **Brown paper:** 24″ × 24″ sheet of thin brown paper*

❋ **3 or 4 patterned papers**

❋ **2 or 3 paper punches:** about 1″–2″ wide (circles, hearts, or any shapes for a special occasion)

❋ **Sequins or buttons**

❋ **Washi tape**

* Use thin paper for the base so that it will fold easily around the present. Brown postal paper is perfect!

Let's Get Making!

1. Using your paper punches, cut shapes from the patterned papers.

2. Put a few rows of washi tape in each direction.

3. ---

Attach the shapes to
the wrapping paper
using a glue stick.

4. -------------------

Using a bright
thread, sew wavy
lines up and down
the paper. Sew over
all the shapes so
they don't fall off.

Tip: Because the paper is
quite big, you will need
to roll it so it fits in your
sewing machine. Adjust the
roll as you sew the wavy
lines so the paper doesn't
tear. Maybe get someone to
help you! You could always
start by making a smaller
one first.

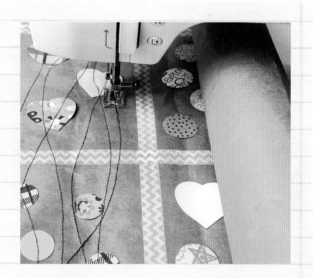

5. Wrap the present.

6. Choose some sequins. Add a tiny amount of white glue to the back of each sequin. Carefully place the sequins where you would like them and leave to dry.

Recycled Gift Bag

Project Supply List

For a list of general sewing supplies, see Basic Supplies (page 14).

❋ **Recycled papers or old books**

❋ **Ribbon:** about 45˝

❋ **Patterned paper for hearts** (Hearts can be cut from recycled items as well.)

Recycled gift bags are such a bargain and unbelievably easy to make. This one is made from an old gardening book; my mum will love it. What are your mum's favorite things? Or your dad's? Brothers, sisters, cousins— what would they get a kick out of seeing their gift come wrapped in? Be creative! Head off to your local second-hand bookstore! Or how about turning some of these items into gift bags: old Christmas and birthday cards, maps, old gift bags, paper bags, or newspaper? Fab idea! Have fun thinking up lots of new wrapping possibilities.

The bag I made is 28˝ long and 13˝ wide, but you can make yours whatever size you like!

Note

Don't rip apart any books without asking an adult first!

Let's Get Making!

1.

Pull out a few sheets of paper from an old book. Trim any ragged edges.

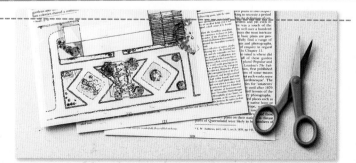

2.

Place 2 sheets together so that they overlap by about 1″. Sew the pages together, about ¼″ from the overlapped edge.

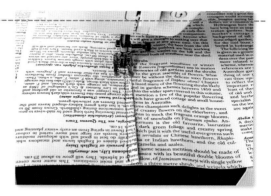

3.

Keep adding and sewing more pages to make a sheet as long and wide as you want. Stitch wherever the pages overlap.

4.

Glue a strip of ribbon all the way down the center. Stitch the ribbon in place using a zigzag stitch.

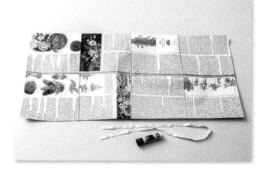

5.

Fold the paper in half, but do not crease it yet. Now slide the side you want to be the back so that it is 2″–4″ longer than the front section. This creates the flap that you will fold over to seal your gift bag. This bag is 3½″ longer at the top.

Front

Back

6.

Fold the back down to make the flap.

Flap

7.

Cut a piece of ribbon long enough to go across the flap. Cut out 5 hearts using the pattern (page 92). Stick the ribbon and hearts to the flap, using a glue stick.

8.

Sew along the ribbon, stitching over the hearts. Unfold your flap so you don't sew your bag closed yet!

9.

Sew the left and right edges of the bag together.

Stitch sides.

10. Pop the present inside the bag and fold the flap back down. If you like, sew across the flap, just below the hearts to seal the bag—so there's no peeking!

Put the present in.

Fold the flap down.

Note

If you want to keep the bag closed, be sure you are sewing through both the flap and the body of the bag.

Sew the flap closed, if you want to.

Refer to Using Tracing Paper and Patterns (page 10) for help with tracing and cutting pattern shapes.

Cut 5 hearts from recycled or patterned paper.

Heart

Bedroom Decor

Canvas Photo Frame

Project Supply List

For a list of general sewing supplies, see Basic Supplies (page 14).

❈ Small stretched canvas

❈ 2 or 3 patterned papers

❈ Paint

❈ Paintbrush

❈ Self-adhesive hook-and-loop tape: 5″ piece

❈ Photograph

We are using hook-and-loop tape in this project, which will mean that you can swap your photos out as often as you like. Pssst— next time, buy a much bigger canvas and make a huge board for several photos. Now that would look awesome!

Tip: For an incredible rainbow of colors, go to your local paint store or hardware store and get tester pots. Take your patterned papers with you and put together a fabulous combination.

Let's Get Making!

1.

After you've picked your color, paint your canvas and let it dry. It may take 2 coats of paint for the color to look its best, so be patient and let each coat of paint dry completely.

Canvas Photo Frame 95

2.

Trace and cut out the toadstools from the patterned papers using the pattern (page 99). You'll need 4 toadstools. With a glue stick, glue all the parts together.

3.

Sew around the edge of each part of the toadstools.

4.

Cut the hook-and-loop tape into 5 pieces, each 1″ long. Keep the hook side and the loop side of the tape together when you cut.

5.

With the hook-and-loop tape together, peel the paper off 1 side of the tape and stick the tape to the back of a toadstool. Do this for all 4 toadstools.

6.

Using the fifth piece of hook-and-loop tape, stick your chosen photo onto the center of your canvas.

7.

Peel away the paper from the hook-and-loop tape on each toadstool so that the sticky side of the tape is facing you, and put the toadstools carefully to the side, with the sticky side up and not touching anything.

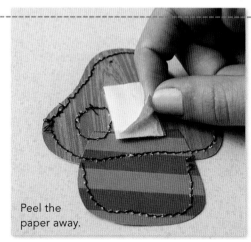

Peel the paper away.

8. Stick the toadstools around the photo so they frame it nicely.

Note

Stick the toadstools to the canvas, not to the photo!

Tips

- You can use a photo that is horizontal or vertical—or choose to turn your photo either way. Remember to make sure your toadstools are turned in the right direction. They don't want to lie down but stand tall. Well, as tall as they can.

- You can make this project even more your own by replacing the toadstools with your own designs, perhaps designs based on the photo you chose. Puppies would have been great in place of the toadstools for my photo!

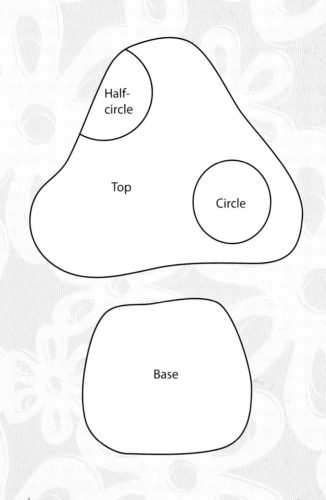

Half-circle

Top

Circle

Base

Refer to Using Tracing Paper and Patterns (page 10) for help with tracing and cutting pattern shapes.

Cut 4 bases, 4 tops, 4 circles, and 4 half-circles from patterned papers.

Difficulty level:

Circle Wallhanging

Brighten up your bedroom with this stunning wallhanging that you made all by yourself. When your friends come to stay over, they will be wowed!

Project Supply List

For a list of general sewing supplies, see Basic Supplies (page 14).

- 1 piece heavyweight patterned card stock
- 3 patterned papers
- Buttons, sequins, or stick-on jewels (diamantés)

Let's Get Making!

1.

Cut a piece of heavyweight patterned card stock 3″ × 12″. Fold in half lengthwise, as in the photo.

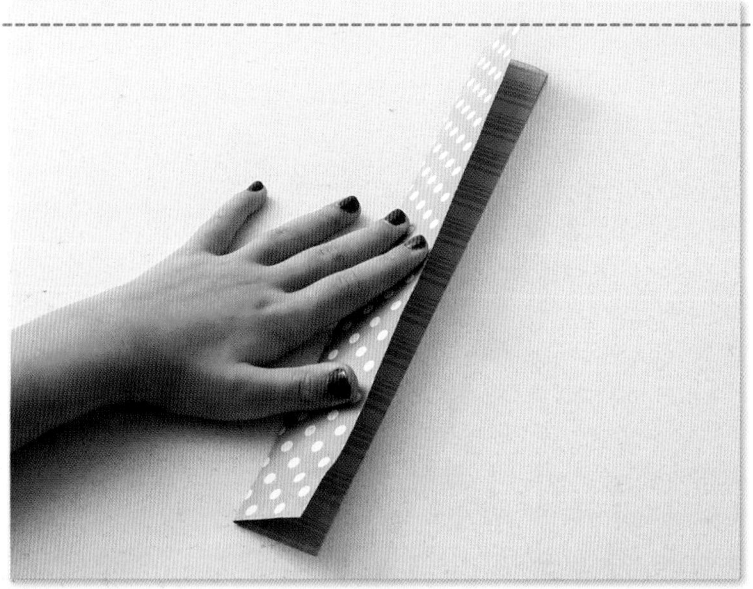

2.

Trace and transfer the circle patterns (page 105) onto different patterned papers. Cut out 44 of the large circles and just 4 of the smaller circles.

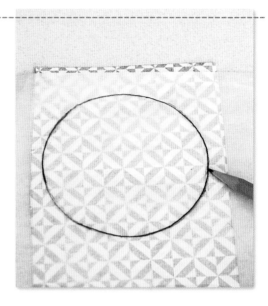

3.

Lay out 1 small and 11 large circles in a vertical row, arranging the circles in any order you like. Put the small circle at the beginning of the row. Make 4 rows, each with 1 small and 11 large circles.

Get ready to sew, slow and steady!

Lay the circles out.

4.

Place the first circle (small) on the sewing machine and sew through the center. Place the second circle (large) so it is slightly overlapping the first circle, and continue sewing. Keep adding, overlapping, and sewing until you have completed the first row of 12.

5.

Sew second and third lines of stitching on this set of circles. Keep the lines of stitching a little bit apart from each other.

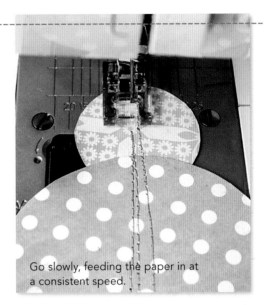

6.

Repeat Steps 4 and 5 until you have finished sewing all 4 rows of circles.

Go slowly, feeding the paper in at a consistent speed.

7.

Open your 12″ folded card stock piece from Step 1 and lay the small circle from each row inside the fold. This will allow the rows of circles to hang from the card. Place the small circles an equal distance apart (it doesn't have to be precise). Glue each of the small circles to the inside of the card stock piece.

8.

Refold the card stock piece and glue it closed. The small circles will be inside the fold.

9.

Sew the folded card stock strip closed. Make sure the circles are on your left as you sew. Sew down the strip a few times to secure the circles and make a pretty design!

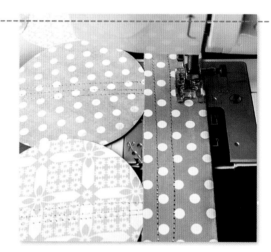

10.

Finish the project by adding some buttons, sequins, or jewels wherever your creative little heart thinks they look good. Use little dabs of white glue to attach the small decorations. Let dry.

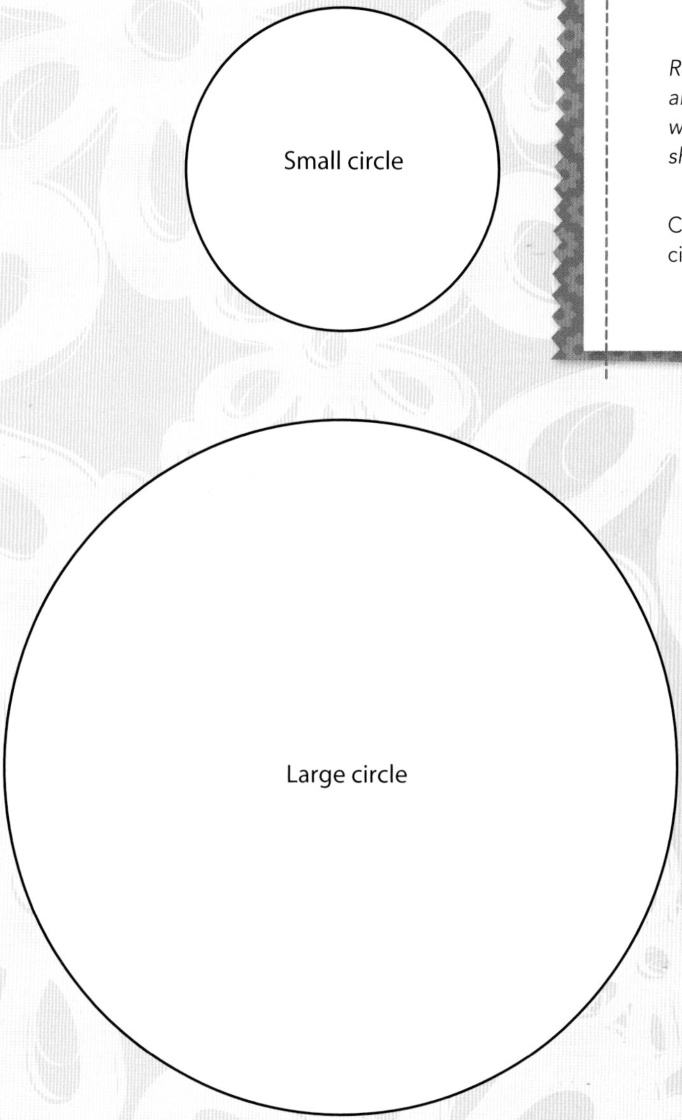

Small circle

Large circle

Refer to Using Tracing Paper and Patterns (page 10) for help with tracing and cutting pattern shapes.

Cut 4 small circles and 44 large circles from patterned papers.

Drink Coaster and Glass Charm

Jazz up a party with this cool drink coaster and matching glass charm! Or just have them lying around your bedroom ready for when your friends pop over. Remember: the coaster is made with vinyl, so cold drinks only, please!

Project Supply List

For a list of general sewing supplies, see Basic Supplies (page 14).

❀ **For drink coaster:**

2 medium-weight patterned papers

2 pieces of vinyl, 6″ × 6″ each

A fun photo

Sequins or sparkly stickers

❀ **For glass charm:**

2 medium-weight patterned papers

10″ piece of narrow ribbon

Hole punch

Sequins or stick-on jewels (diamantés)

Let's Get Making!

Drink Coaster

1.

Trace and cut out a large circle, a large heart, and a small heart (page 111) from some gorgeous patterned papers. Stick them together, using a glue stick. Sew around the shapes, as shown.

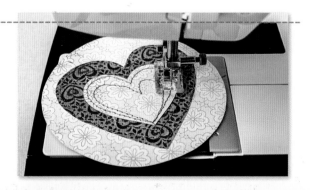

2. Trace and cut out another large circle from your papers.

3. Trace the small circle (see patterns, page 111) around 1 of your favorite photos. Cut out the photo and glue it to the center of the large circle that you cut out in Step 2. Sew around the edge of the photo.

4.

Place the 2 large circles (1 with hearts and the other with a photo) together back to back. The photo and hearts should be on the outside. Glue together with a glue stick, then stitch around the outer edge.

5. Place a piece of vinyl on either side of the circles, and sew carefully around the edge of the large circles again. Trim off any extra vinyl so it looks tidy.

6.

Add some sequins to the outside edge of the coaster.

Finished! Sort of. It seems lonely, that one little coaster. Maybe the glass charm will help.

Glass Charm

1. Cut out 2 small circles and 2 small hearts, using the patterns (page 111). Glue a heart to each of the circles and carefully sew around. Stick the circles together back to back and stitch around to finish it off.

2.
Punch a small hole through the top.

3.
Thread through some lovely soft ribbon in a matching color, add some bling with a few sequins or jewels, and ta-da!

Now you have a drink coaster and a glass charm, beautiful, matching, and personalized. However, one pair is not a party. Coasters and charms usually come in sets of at least four. So ... make more! Then let's have a party!

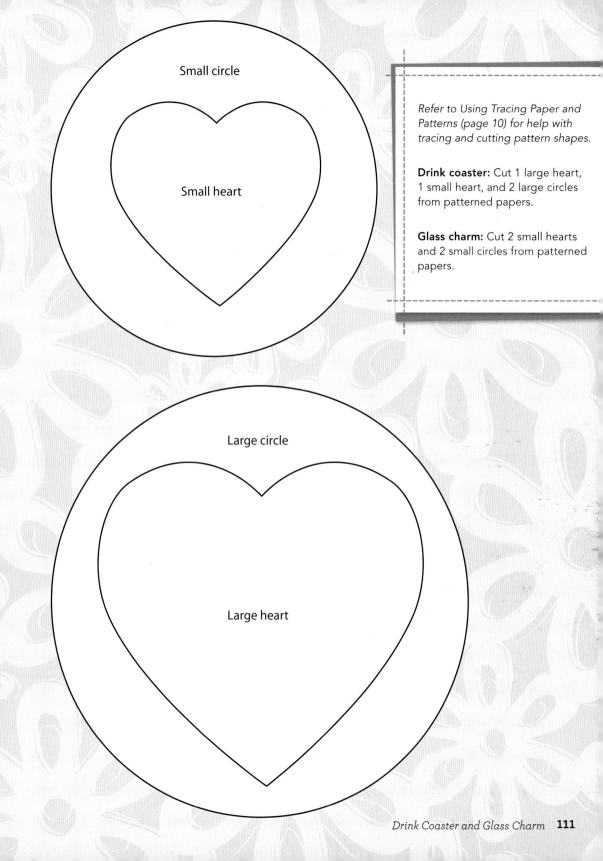

Small circle

Small heart

Large circle

Large heart

Refer to *Using Tracing Paper and Patterns* (page 10) for help with tracing and cutting pattern shapes.

Drink coaster: Cut 1 large heart, 1 small heart, and 2 large circles from patterned papers.

Glass charm: Cut 2 small hearts and 2 small circles from patterned papers.

Framed Owl Art

These stitched pieces of art will look fabulous hanging in your bedroom. Grab yourself a fresh white frame to pop it in, and it will look unique!

Project Supply List

For a list of general sewing supplies, see Basic Supplies (page 14).

❋ **Heavy, plain white card stock:** an 8″ × 10″ piece (A) and a 7½″ × 9½″ piece (B)

❋ **4–5 patterned papers for owl shapes**

❋ **2 buttons:** about ½″ wide each

❋ **Picture frame:** 8″ × 10″

Let's Get Making!

1. Trace around each part of the owl pattern (page 115) and cut out the pieces from patterned papers.

2. Glue the owl pieces onto the middle of card stock piece B (7½″ × 9½″).

3. Sew around the parts of the owl and trim off any loose threads. Sew around the eyes a few times to make them really stand out.

4. Stick card stock piece B to card stock piece A, using a glue stick.

5. Rethread the sewing machine with white thread. Don't forget to change thread in the bobbin, too! Sew all the way around the edge of card stock B. Try to keep your stitches straight.

Tips

- When sticking card stock piece B to card stock piece A, just dab the glue, but make sure you cover the whole area. This will stop lumps of glue from showing through to your finished artwork.

- When sticking one card stock piece to another, lay them in place and then put a piece of paper on top. Press down firmly with the palm of your hand. This will prevent air bubbles.

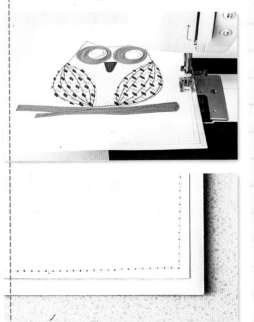

6. Dab a little bit of white glue on the backs of the buttons. Place them in the centers of the eyes and leave them to dry.

7. Put your artwork in a picture frame.

Adorable! How wise of you.

Refer to Using Tracing Paper and Patterns (page 10) for help with tracing and cutting pattern shapes.

Cut 1 of each shape from patterned papers.

Owl

Heart Bunting

Project Supply List

For a list of general sewing supplies, see Basic Supplies (page 14).

❀ **4–5 patterned papers**

❀ **Ribbon:** 2 pieces each about 15˝ long

❀ **Hole punch**

I love this paper bunting; it's just so pretty. You can easily put your own stamp on this project, too! For a longer banner, you could cut lots of smaller hearts. Add some glitzy jewels. If you make lots of them, they would be great decorations for a birthday party!

Let's Get Making!

1. Trace the heart pattern (page 119) onto different patterned papers, and cut out. You will need 15 hearts altogether.

Tip: If you have a heart-shaped paper cutter of a similar size, use that. It will save you so much time.

2.

Lay the hearts out on a table so you can figure out where they will look best. Try not to have 2 of the same pattern together.

3.

Measure ½˝ down from the center of a heart and make a small pencil mark. Do this to all 15 hearts.

4.

Place the first heart on the sewing machine, and slowly stitch across in a straight line, going through the pencil mark you made.

5.

Place the second heart so it slightly overlaps the first heart. Keep sewing in a straight line. Make sure you sew through the pencil mark again. Repeat until you have sewn through all 15 hearts. Trim off any loose threads.

6.

Repeat Step 5, but start about ¼˝ to the left of the first stitched line. This will make your heart bunting sturdy and really pretty at the same time! Stitch another row so that you have 3 stitched lines.

7.

Punch a hole in each end of the bunting and add some lovely soft ribbon so you can tie up your gorgeous bunting!

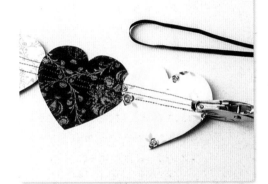

Heart

Refer to Using Tracing Paper and Patterns (page 10) for help with tracing and cutting pattern shapes.

Cut 15 hearts from patterned papers.

Camper Van Bunting

Project Supply List

For a list of general sewing supplies, see Basic Supplies (page 14).

❊ 3 patterned papers

❊ 1 solid-color paper

❊ 24 buttons: about ½˝ wide

❊ Twine or narrow ribbon: 2½ yards

❊ Hole punch

I want you to be really creative with your sewing for this fabulous camper van project. It doesn't have to be perfect—quirky is OK. When choosing the papers, think bright, cheerful, and colorful! Imagine you're at the beach. Think sun, sand, sea, colorful umbrellas, swimming suits, and ice cream.

Let's Get Making!

1. Trace and cut out each section of the camper van pattern (page 123). Cut enough pieces to make 12 vans, using various papers so each van will be unique.

2. Use a glue stick to glue the pieces together for each van—12 vans in total!

Isn't it cool how the vans are all different?

Yet they go together like family.

GIFTS TO MAKE

- CAITLYN: BOOKMARK
- LUCY: FRAME
- SADIE: NOTE BOOK
- OLIVIA: NECKLACE
- EMMA: TOTE BAG

TO DO:
1. PACK FOR CAMP
2. GET NEW SWIMSUIT
3. ~~MOM ABOUT CELL PHONE~~
4. CLEAN ROOM

To: Ashley

3.

With bright-colored thread, sew around each van. You could sew all of the van, or if you want, you could just sew parts of it—it's up to you!

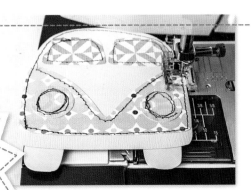

Well done! You now have the 12 vans all lined up and stitched. Phew!

4.

Punch a hole on each side of each van, just above the circle headlights. That's 2 holes per van.

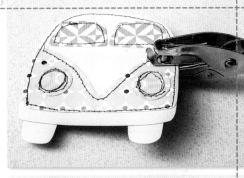

5.

Cut a piece of twine or ribbon about 6″ long. Thread it through a hole in the first van and then through the hole of the van next to it. Leave about 1″ between the vans so they hang nicely. Knot the twine and trim the ends.

6.

Attach all of your vans this way, so they form a long row. You will need to cut 10 more 6″ pieces of twine or ribbon to keep them together.

And now for the finish!

7. Cut 2 pieces of twine or ribbon about 8″ each. Tie these through the holes at either end of your row of vans, so you can hang your bunting.

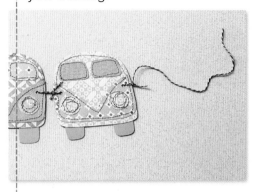

8. With a little dab of white glue, attach a button in the center of each headlight.

Gorgeous!

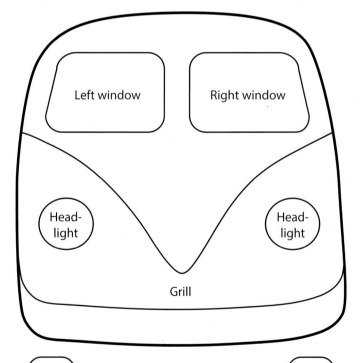

Left window

Right window

Head-light

Head-light

Grill

Tire

Tire

Refer to Using Tracing Paper and Patterns (page 10) for help with tracing and cutting pattern shapes.

Cut 12 camper vans (using bold lines), 12 left windows, 12 right windows, 12 grills, 24 headlights, and 24 tires from solid-colored and patterned papers.

Just a Few
More Ideas

Photos by Ali Benyon

Don't stop now just because you've reached the end of the book. There are many, many different ways to apply this great idea of stitching into paper! With the variety of paper, threads, and embellishments out there, you could turn your hand to almost anything you put your mind to. Here are a few more of the paper-stitched designs I have made. I hope these will spark more ideas for you! Stitch away, my friends! Stitch away!

Stitched Paper Art for Kids

About the Author

A surface pattern designer originally from the United Kingdom, Ali Benyon is the crafty brains behind two successful businesses, Ali Benyon Designs and Cheeky Pickle (alibenyondesigns.com.au and cheekypickle.com.au). Using bold shapes and unique mark-making techniques, her designs are contemporary, fresh, and vibrant. She is passionate about injecting color, pattern, and texture into each of her designs.

She is a very enthusiastic writer and has written many articles about the handmade industry. She loves writing for her own blog as well!

Ali now lives by the sea on the Mornington Peninsula in Australia, with her small family—husband Dave, children Madeleine and Greta, and two cheeky but very adorable dogs, Dougal and Rosie.

Ali
Benyon